CONTENTS

 Whenever you see this sign in this book it means there are some more details at the FOOT of the page, like here.

The **SECRET** Life of...
VICTORIA

WITHDRAWN

Bob Fowke

Hodder
Children's
Books

A division of Hodder Headline Limited

Hello!
I'm the Artful Dodger!
Come with me and you'll find out
about Victoria and her posh friends – and
all about life with my mates at the poor end of
the street.

I'm a champion pickpocket! I get to know a lot about
people (both rich and poor), and what they get up
to. Nothing escapes me.

Produced by Lazy Summer Books for Hodder Children's Books

This edition published by Hodder Children's Books, 2005

10 9 8 7 6 5 4 3 2 1

ISBN 0340 88423 1

The paper and board used in this paperback are natural recyclable products made from wood grown in sustainable forests. The manufacturing processes conform to the environmental regulations of the country of origin.

Hodder Children's Books
a division of Hodder Headline Limited
338 Euston Road
London NW1 3BH
Printed and bound by Bookmarque Ltd, Croydon, Surrey
A Catalogue record for this book is available from the British Library

LITTLE FAT QUEEN

SHE RULED THE WORLD

June 2nd 1897. It's hot and clammy. A short, fat, old woman leans back in her carriage and opens a black lace parasol. Outside, the streets are lined with thousands and thousands of people, all cheering madly.

Queen Victoria, Empress of India, the most powerful woman in the world, has been Queen for sixty years. This is her Diamond Jubilee. She's hot and the noise is deafening. She needs a cup of tea – with a dash of whisky. She sighs. She had more energy when she became Queen. Sixty years ago she was a lively girl of eighteen. Now look at her...

PROFILE OF VICTORIA AGED 78

JOB	Queen
HEIGHT	Under five feet
WIDTH	Around five feet
EYESIGHT	Poor
HAIR	Grey
PERSONALITY	A bit gloomy
FAVOURITE COLOUR	Black

Let's find out how it all began.....

A LONG SHOT

Victoria was part of a family of Germans, mainly called George, who came from Hanover. From 1760, Mad King George III ruled for sixty years and had fifteen children.

Victoria was the only daughter of Mad King George the III's third son, the Duke of Kent. It's amazing she got to the throne at all, as her two drunken uncles, Kings George IV and William IV, had a total of thirteen children. But the whole lot died young or were illegitimate (their mother and father weren't married) so they didn't count.

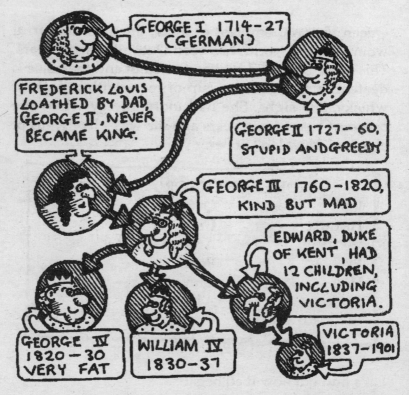

GEORGE I 1714 – 27 (GERMAN)

FREDERICK LOUIS LOATHED BY DAD, GEORGE II, NEVER BECAME KING.

GEORGE II 1727 – 60, STUPID AND GREEDY

GEORGE III 1760 – 1820, KIND BUT MAD

EDWARD, DUKE OF KENT, HAD 12 CHILDREN, INCLUDING VICTORIA.

GEORGE IV 1820 – 30 VERY FAT

WILLIAM IV 1830 – 37

VICTORIA 1837 – 1901

JUST IN TIME

In March, 1819, on the road from Germany to the French coast, a carriage swayed and bounced along pot-holed roads. The driver, a fat, balding man with long sideburns, whipped the horses to hurry up.

The driver was the Duke of Kent, too poor to hire a coachman. Inside was the Duchess of Kent, eight months pregnant. Why the hurry? Well, a gypsy had told the Duke that his child would rule England. The worry was that the child might be born in Germany or France. To be Queen of England, it would help if she was born on the right side of the English Channel.

The Duke of Kent, was once described as "the greatest rascal that ever went unhung". He was the most hated man in the British army, which was quite something. He once caused a mutiny on Gibraltar when he closed the wine-shops.

They made it to England in time. Baby Victoria was born on 24th May, 1819, in Kensington Palace, London. Eight months later the Duke died, leaving the Duchess and tiny Victoria almost penniless.

THE AGE IS NAMED

Fat George IV was jealous. He didn't want the Kents' baby to have a state christening, so he made it as difficult as he could. The Duke of Kent had chosen five names:

Victoria (after her mother)

Georgina (after the king)

Alexandrina (after the Tsar of Russia)

Charlotte (after Fat George's dead daughter)

Augusta (as a good royal name).

Fat George objected to the list. At the ceremony, when the Archbishop of Canterbury said, "Name this child," Fat George just replied "Alexandrina".

WAAA!

There was an embarrassed pause. What about the other names? The Duke of Kent got in a fluster. "Elizabeth!" he said. Fat George shook his head. None of the usual royal names were to be used.

The Duchess of Kent burst into tears and everybody looked hot or angry. In the end the baby was named Alexandrina Victoria, with Victoria the preferred name. It was a close thing. The great Victorian Age might have been called something completely different!

CHILDHOOD AND SKOOL

GROWING UP GRIM

Young Princess Victoria was fair-haired, blue-eyed and podgy. Her first language was German. At three she learned English and then French. Later, she learned Hindustani because she was the ruler of India as well. Some people say she spoke English with a German accent.

As she grew older Victoria started to throw tantrums. Her governess said she had never before seen such a naughty child. Victoria wasn't told she might be Queen until she was eleven years old. She was made to sleep in her mother's room and was never left alone. To make herself look taller she learned to keep her head up straight by wearing a sprig of holly tucked into the neck of her dress.

Victoria and other aristocratic children were taught at home. This meant they were brought up for a life of leisure. They were expected to be well-read, religious and good at embroidery, which was all very nice, but what happened to everyone else?...

SCHOOLS FOR GIRLS

At the start of Victoria's reign, there were a few voluntary schools. But from 1880, everyone had to have at least some schooling, although few women went to secondary school.

People thought that girls only needed to learn things to help them be good wives, mothers and servants. German girls, for example, learned the '3 Ks' – Kinder, Kuche, Kirche (children, cooking, church).

Most upper class girls were only taught music, dancing, drawing and sewing. Some learned to balance heavy books on their heads whilst walking around the room. This was to help them learn deportment.

There were a few academies. These were boarding schools which promised to teach girls subjects like Latin, history and geography but the heads were more interested in taking the fees than in teaching. Upper class girls were expected to marry wealthy husbands, who would not want their wives to work. Unmarried girls might get a job as a governess. Things were different for boys...

 Good deportment meant walking in an elegant way, with the head and held high.

SCHOOLS FOR BOYS

Rich middle class boys got packed off to painfully posh public schools. They lived in the schools as boarders, and conditions could be very strict.

They learnt Latin and Greek parrot-fashion, (just repeating everything until it sticks in your mind). They sat on forms (long wooden benches) in form rooms. Conditions were horrible. There weren't enough teachers to control the boys and much bullying went on. There were cases of boys being burned with cigar ends or roasted in front of fires by bigger boys.

The teachers could be just as brutal. The headmaster of Eton once flogged seventy-two boys in one session. Dr Philips, the principal at Cheltenham School, once caned a runaway boy so severely that his jacket was cut to pieces. The boy spent three days in bed recovering!

Things got better slowly. At Rugby, headmaster Dr Thomas Arnold turned a rough-house into a model school. It was here that one boy, William Webb Ellis, picked up the ball during a soccer game and invented the game of rugby!

FOUR FEARSOME FACTS ABOUT VICTORIAN SCHOOLS:

1. Some teachers couldn't read or write; some couldn't even sign their own names.

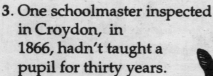

2. In 1845, a deaf hunchback was given a job as a teacher in Yorkshire, so that the parish wouldn't have to keep him as a pauper.

3. One schoolmaster inspected in Croydon, in 1866, hadn't taught a pupil for thirty years.

4. Punishing children was often considered as important as teaching them! The schoolmaster at Whittlesford, Cambridgeshire, was a one-armed ex-sailor called Joshua Macer. He beat his boys with a whip which he called 'Old Hagger', holding them between his knees. The boys bit his legs as they were held and his white stockings were stained with blood.

OUT OF SCHOOL

Away from school, children might have toys to play with. Of course, not everyone could afford the more expensive items.

Dolls
Slate and chalks
Hoop and stick
Spinning top
Hobby horse
Rocking horse
Ice skates

Wooden sailing boat
Lead soldiers
Soap (for blowing bubbles)
Cricket bat
More chalk (for hopscotch)
and marbles...

Most poor children had to work and were too tired to play. In any case, they lived in crowded conditions and had nowhere to play indoors. Things were different for Victoria...

A POSH CHILDHOOD

When Victoria was young, she liked having fun. She liked going to the seaside, dressing up, dancing and playing with her dog, Dash.

She loved the ballet and going to see pantomimes and plays, as well as opera. Everywhere she went, with her mother and her mother's fancy man Sir John Conroy in tow, she was cheered by crowds. Victoria liked men, including her German cousins . Her diary has lots about her cousin Albert. She really fancied him

 Victoria was part of a vast network of cousins who ruled most of Europe, including Germany and Russia. Her favourite uncle was Leopold, King of the Belgians.

 Sex, or even petting, outside marriage – apart from a chaste kiss – was considered shocking in respectable circles.

WAKE UP DEAR, YOU'RE QUEEN!

GET OUT OF THE WAY MUM

King William IV died early in the morning of 20th June, 1837 at Windsor. Straight away, the Archbishop of Canterbury and two others drove hot-foot over to Kensington Palace to tell Victoria the news. There was nobody to tell, not at five in the morning. They had to hammer on the door for ages before sleepy servants let them in. It took another age to waken the Duchess, who took another half an hour to shake her daughter. Finally, Victoria appeared, a childish figure in a dressing gown and slippers, her hair untidy with sleep. The three grand messengers fell to their knees and kissed her hand.

A month past her eighteenth birthday, plump Victoria became Queen of England. Her mother was cross, especially when Victoria ordered her bed to be taken out of her mother's room. Later, when Victoria moved into Buckingham Palace, she banished her mother to a far wing. The Duchess spent the rest of her life being a disagreeable old woman and giving the servants a hard time.

CORONATION CAPERS

The coronation was fixed for 28th June, 1838; one year into Victoria's reign and just over a month past her nineteenth birthday. Victoria slept badly the night before, not helped by the cannons which started booming at four in the morning. It had rained all night but when she stepped into the State Coach, the sun shone. It seemed the sun shone whenever Victoria went anywhere. It can't have done, but that didn't stop people calling sunshine 'The Queen's Weather'.

Parliament coughed up £200,000 for the coronation. Westminster Abbey was decorated in crimson and gold, a huge two-day fair was held in Hyde Park and there were fireworks and bands in all the royal parks.

About half a million people crowded the streets as the Queen set off for Westminister Abbey at dead on ten o'clock. The Abbey was like a treasure chest with gold and jewels everywhere. One guest, Prince Esterhazy, looked as if he had been 'caught out in a rain of diamonds and come in dripping'.

Then things started to go wrong...

MORE REHEARSALS, NEXT TIME

✡ The coronation robe, stiff with gold, was too big and too heavy for the tiny Queen.

✡ The Archbishop of Canterbury crushed the ring onto the Queen's wrong finger.

✡ The Bishop of Durham gave her the Orb too soon and she nearly dropped it.

✡ The Bishop of Bath and Wells turned over two pages in the prayer book by mistake, telling the Queen that the ceremony was over when it wasn't.

✡ Baron John Rolle lived up to his name when he fell over as he made a bow and rolled back down the steps.

✡ The altar of St Edward's Chapel was littered with sandwiches and bottles of wine as the grandees tucked into snacks.

THE DIABOLICAL DOCTOR

The first scandal of Victoria's reign involved an incompetent doctor, a sick lady and her rascally friend called Conway.

The lady was Flora Hastings, Lady-in-Waiting to Victoria's mum. The doctor was called Clark.

Doctor Clark couldn't tell one end of a stethoscope from another. He had once wrongly diagnosed Victoria as being bilious ☚, *when really she had typhoid.*

Lady Flora's stomach swelled up suddenly. Rumour was that she was pregnant by her friend Conroy, who was known to fancy the ladies. Doctor Clark could not help her and Lady Flora died. It turned out she was suffering from cancer of the liver.

The papers went to town, claiming she had been done away with to protect the royal household from a scandal.

👣 Bilious means having too much bile in your system. Bile is a fluid produced by the liver to help digestion, but having too much of it will make you ill.

DATE-A-MATE

The scandal over Lady Flora wasn't a very good start to Victoria's reign, and there were other problems such as high food prices and unemployment. Nasty rumours about Victoria started to spead.

It was said that something was going on between Victoria and Lord Melbourne, the Prime Minister. People started shouting "Mrs Melbourne" at her whenever she went out.

Something had to be done – quickly. A Royal wedding seemed like a good way to take people's minds off things. Victoria had to choose a mate. The possibles were:

1. GEORGE, DUKE OF CAMBRIDGE
   He had a bad complexion,
   hidden by whiskers.
   He had very pushy parents.
   Melbourne didn't like him.

2. GEORGE, DUKE OF CUMBERLAND
   He suddenly went blind.
   He became King of Hanover.

3. ALBERT, PRINCE OF SAXE-COBURG
   Handsome.
   Musical and technical.

Guess who won?

FALLING IN LOVE

Victoria fancied Albert because:	Albert fancied Victoria because:
He was handsome. He looked rather weak and ill sometimes (he kept falling asleep in company) and she wanted to look after him. He was very dependable and sincere.	She was Queen of about a quarter of the world. She adored him. She thought he was always right.

Things began to get serious on 10th November 1839, although the day did not begin well: a madman broke lots of windows at Windsor Castle; Victoria and Prime Minister Melbourne both felt unwell after eating pork at dinner the night before; Prince Albert had been sea-sick on the ferry from Europe.

Albert had come over to see if Victoria would marry him. Victoria found him very attractive. She wrote about him:

> Such beautiful blue eyes, an exquisite nose and a pretty mouth with delicate moustache and slight, but very slight whiskers, a beautiful figure, broad in the shoulders and a fine waist.

On the third evening, when Prince Albert was bidding her goodnight with a shake of her hand, he gave it a special squeeze! They got engaged the next day. However Victoria had to propose to Albert as no one could ask to marry the Queen.

A NAME FOR ALBERT

In 1840, Victoria and Albert got married. But others were not so keen on this stiff German. What to call Albert was a problem. Look at the options:

'King' was not acceptable. Albert was a no-good German and this would mean that a German family could take over Britain.

Victoria suggested 'King Consort', but there never had been a King Consort. It needed special Parliamentary permission.

It was decided not even to make him a lord. Prince or not, the English lords did not feel a German could be their equal.

In the end, poor old Albert had to stick with his German title of Prince of Saxe-Coburg. In 1854, however, after the success of the Great Exhibition, he got the title 'Prince Consort'.

ALBERT TAKES CHARGE

Like all married couples, Victoria and Albert sometimes quarrelled. Soon after their marriage Albert stalked out of the room after a disagreement and locked himself in his apartments. Victoria hammered on the door. "Who's there?" Albert asked. When Victoria answered, "The Queen of England," he refused to answer the door. The second time this happened, Albert still refused to open up. On the third time, when Albert asked, "Who's there?" Victoria humbly answered, "Your wife, Albert." He opened the door at once.

There would be some changes from now on.

- ☞ They would live in the country.
- ☞ Albert would run the palace and its accounts, which were in a mess.
- ☞ Albert would dance with Victoria, as long as she stopped at midnight.

HAPPY FAMILIES

Victoria came to be known as 'the Grandmother of Europe'. Her children were to sit on many a royal throne. She couldn't stand having babies but she did it nine times in all.

- In her first year of marriage, Victoria, the Princess Royal, was born. She later became Empress of Germany and mother of Kaiser Bill, who took Europe into the first First World War.

- In 1841, less than a year later, came 'Bertie', the Prince of Wales, later King Edward VII.

Her other children were:

- ALICE, later Grand Duchess of Hesse
- ALFRED, later Duke of Edinburgh
- HELENA, later Princess Christian of Schleswig-Holstein.

- LOUISE, to be Duchess of Argyle
- ARTHUR, Duke of Connaught
- LEOPOLD, Duke of Albany
- BEATRICE, later Princess Henry of Battenberg

By 1860, when the last of the royal babies had come into the world, Victoria had been Queen for twenty-three years. What people didn't know was that she had another forty-one years to go!

FIVE THINGS YOU DIDN'T KNOW ABOUT VICTORIA

1. Victoria and Albert were in the habit of privately exchanging nude pictures.

2. The Queen loved to travel in disguise and to be mistaken for somebody else. Once when she was in disguise Old Lord Portarlington once greeted her with the words, "I know your face quite well, but dammit I cannot put a name to it."

3. One moonlit night, Victoria was looking out of the window at Windsor when she was chatted-up by the sentry below, who mistook her for a housemaid. This made the Queen laugh so much she felt sick.

4. The Queen loved rings. She had plump hands with rings on every finger and even on her thumbs. She could barely pick up her knife and fork whilst eating at a dinner given by the Emperor of France in 1855.

5. Victoria hated cigar smoke. Most of Victoria's sons smoked cigars, so they set up a secret smoking-room. Victoria heard about it and planned to search the whole of Windsor Castle to find it. Panic reigned until Bertie, the Prince of Wales, thought to put up a WC notice over the door.

WC stands for Water Closet, an old word for the lavatory.

THE GREAT TRADE SHOW

A WONDERFUL GREENHOUSE

The Great Exhibition of 1851 was the biggest trade show in the world, and Prince Albert made it happen. There are few people better able to twist arms or request favours than the Queen's hubby.

The site, in Hyde Park, was chosen by Albert himself. The top people who lived there were not best pleased. They feared the place would be over-run by 'the Great Unwashed' (how they thought of common people).

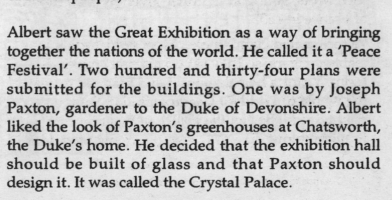

Albert saw the Great Exhibition as a way of bringing together the nations of the world. He called it a 'Peace Festival'. Two hundred and thirty-four plans were submitted for the buildings. One was by Joseph Paxton, gardener to the Duke of Devonshire. Albert liked the look of Paxton's greenhouses at Chatsworth, the Duke's home. He decided that the exhibition hall should be built of glass and that Paxton should design it. It was called the Crystal Palace.

The Crystal Palace

Some amazing facts about the Crystal Palace:

- ✿ it covered about 4 kilometres square of ground
- ✿ it measured 564 metres in length
- ✿ it contained 4,572 tonnes of iron
- ✿ it contained almost 300,000 panes of glass
- ✿ it used twenty-four miles of guttering
- ✿ it held 14,000 displays
- ✿ and attracted more than six million visitors.

All sorts of objections were raised against the building: glass panes would be shattered by hailstones; a gust of wind would blow it down; galleries would fall in and kill visitors.

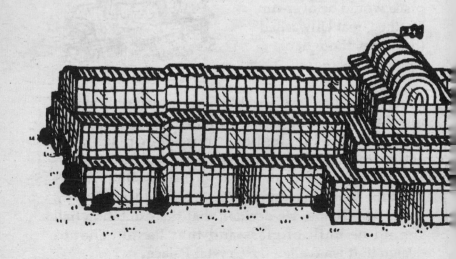

One big worry was that the exhibits would be covered in sparrow droppings. The sparrows couldn't be shot because that would break the glass. No solutions were found to keep the sparrows away until the elderly Duke of Wellington suggested to Victoria, "Sparrow-hawks, Ma'am".

Exhibits were divided into four parts: raw materials, mechanical inventions, manufacturers, and works of art. Visitors gazed in wonder at the exhibits, which included giant steam engines, a massive diamond called the Koh-i-Noor, a garden seat made from coal, champagne made from rhubarb and a loom from a textile mill.

The Great Exhibition of 1851 was Albert's finest moment and Victoria was as pleased as Punch.

FANTASTIC FIRSTS

The Great Exhibition was a great show-case for Victorian achievements. There were plenty of them during her reign. Here are fifteen fantastic firsts from before, during, and after the Great Exhibition:

- ✿ RUBBER ELASTIC was first made in France in 1830 by British workmen. The Victorians soon began to use it for underwear.

- ✿ In 1840 Britain introduced the first pre-paid POSTAGE STAMP. Called the Penny Black (because it was black and cost a penny), it replaced the old system when the receiver of a letter had to pay the cost of the postage.

- ✿ The first PUBLIC LAVATORIES in London were opened in 1852. They were a flop, and closed after a month, probably because it cost two pence (one penny in today's money) for the use of basic amenities and another two pence for washing your hands – a lot of money then. An unskilled labourer had to live on half a crown (12½ pence) a day – including rent.

- ✿ The first CHRISTMAS CARD was designed in 1843 by John Calcott Horsley. He later became famous for his campaign against the use of nude models by artists. This earned him the nickname 'Clothes-Horsley'.

- The first BOWLER HAT was made in 1849 by the firm of Thomas and William Bowler of London. It was made for a Norfolk farmer who tested it out by stamping on it. Although popularly known as a 'Bowler', hat makers still to this day prefer to call it a 'Coke', or 'Billy-Cock', from the name of the farmer who first ordered it.

- Although we often complain about the state of our roads, spare a thought for the early Victorians. They had to suffer cobbles or just plain mud pot-holes. But help was at hand. In 1845, London Road, Nottingham, became the first road to be covered with TARMACADAM or TARMAC.

- The first chocolate EASTER EGGS were made by Fry's of Bristol in 1875. This was a new twist to the custom of giving eggs at Easter.

- The first man to swim the ENGLISH CHANNEL was Captain Matthew Webb in August 1875. It took him twenty-two hours. Webb learned to swim in a local canal near his home in Dawley, Shropshire. He later drowned whilst trying to swim beneath the Niagara Falls.

- Have you ever tried to find a number in a TELEPHONE DIRECTORY? It was easier in 1880. Britain's first directory, published by The London Telephone Company, was only six pages long. The telephone had been invented by Scotsman Alexander Graham Bell in America in 1876.

- In Nelson, Lancashire, an Austrian called Herr Steinbeck made the world's first JELLY BABIES in 1864, though Victorians had to wait until 1899 for the first LIQUORICE ALLSORTS.

- The London Metropolitan Railway, opened in 1863 was the first UNDERGROUND RAILWAY in the world built to carry passengers. The name Metropolitan (or Metro) was adopted by other cities for their underground railways.

- SOAP became popular when the Duke of Wellington set the trend among wealthier Victorians for having a daily bath. The first wrapped soap was sold in 1829 as James Atkinson's Old Brown London Soap .

- The first LION TAMER was 'Manchester Jack', lion keeper at Wombwell's Menagerie, a travelling show that toured England. His first act, performed in 1835, consisted of sitting on the back of an elderly lion called Nero and prising open his jaws.

GRRR...

- The first TRAFFIC SIGNS in Britain were erected in 1879 to warn cyclists of dangerous hills. They read: TO CYCLISTS – THIS HILL IS DANGEROUS. Other warning signs included the skull-and-crossbones!

GETTING THERE NO 1 - THE RAILWAYS

Many of the people who flocked to the Great Exhibition came by rail. The first public steam railway from Stockton to Darlington had been opened in 1825.

In 1829, a competition for the best railway engine was won by the Rocket, built by George Stephenson. A year later, the first city-to-city line opened between Liverpool and Manchester. George and his son Robert were also responsible for the width between tracks, which in 1846 was fixed by law at 4'8" (143.51cm).

First-class rail travel was more comfortable, quicker and cheaper than stage coach. A four-day coach journey from York to London took only twelve hours by train.

The 1840s was a time of railway madness. Trains were cheap, fast and seemed to offer easy money for investors. Railway companies sprang up like mushrooms. Many companies were crooked and stole investors' savings. But by the end of the century, there was scarcely a town without a railway station.

Railways were built by navvies (or navigators, to give them their posh name). With pick, shovel, wheelbarrow and dynamite (a Victorian invention), they blasted tunnels and built embankments and bridges. They wore fancy waistcoats and moleskin trousers and had names like 'Fighting Joe'

and 'Gypsy Jack.' They had a terrible reputation for boozing and brawling. Gangs of British navvies helped also to build the railways of France.

Not everybody liked the railways. Farmers claimed that the noise and steam would cause their cows' milk to dry up. Landowners charged fortunes to allow the railways to cross their land, and wanted expensive viaducts to be built because they looked prettier than cheaper embankments.

Eton College, the famous school, forbade the Great Western Railway to build a station at Slough, but the company was too clever for them. They didn't build a station but trains stopped there anyway. Tickets were sold at a nearby pub.

SAFETY FIRST
Travellers' handbooks advised men to guard their wallets in tunnels. They even suggested that women put pins in their mouths to avoid being kissed in the dark!

THE FIRST RAILWAY ACCIDENT

Many important people were invited to go on the first journey of the new Liverpool to Manchester railway in 1830, including actress Fanny Kemble and Member of Parliament, Charles Huskisson. There were about eight hundred people aboard. This is Huskisson's story, as told by Fanny Kemble:

"The engine had stopped to take on a supply of water and several of the gentlemen in the directors' carriage jumped out to look about them, when an engine on the other line, which was parading up and down merely to show its speed, was seen coming down upon them like lightning. The most active of those in peril sprung back into their seats. Mr Huskisson, less active from the effects of age and ill-health, bewildered too by the frantic cries of "Stop the engine!" and "Clear the track!" which resounded on all sides, completely lost his head, looked helplessly to the right and left, and was instantaneously prostrated by the fatal machine, which was dashed down like a thunderbolt upon him, and passed over his leg, smashing and mangling it in the most horrible way."

They bandaged Huskisson up and took him in the engine to Manchester, but he died the same day, the first victim of a passenger rail accident.

GETTING THERE NO 2 – THE OMNIBUS

To get from the station to the Great Exhibition, or to travel there from other parts of London, many people would have taken a bus. The idea of the omnibus was French, and came to London in 1829. The early buses were horse-drawn. They had straw on the floor and garden benches for seats. The top deck had no roof.

The conductor stood at the back and dragged passengers aboard as the bus passed. It picked people up from both sides of the street, zig-zagging as it went.

By the 1860s, Victorians who could afford it travelled on a 'knifeboard' omnibus. Passengers sat back to back on long wooden benches that ran the length of the bus. The sides were open so their legs could be seen from the street. Such travel was thought unladylike, so the top deck was for men only.

GETTING THERE NO 3 – THE TRAMCAR

Horse-pulled tramcars ran on fixed rails. American G. F. Train brought them to Britain. Later, in 1891,

In fact the Victorians were excessively delicate about women's legs in general. In extreme cases they even covered up the legs of pianos and other furniture.

34

electric, trams began to drive the tram-horses off the streets. The trams helped working people to travel. Instead of just drinking in local pubs and gin palaces, they could travel to music halls and the theatre.

GETTING THERE NO 4 - THE STEAMSHIP

At the time of the Great Exhibition, steam ships were just starting to take over from sail. A few years later, in 1858, the Great Eastern, designed by Isambard Kingdom Brunel was launched. She was a paddle-steamer with a screw propeller, and six times bigger than any other ship then afloat. A boiler burst shortly after launching and killed six men.

The Great Eastern never carried as many people as she was meant to. One reason was her ghost. Unexplained tapping noises could be heard in all sorts of weather. Repeated searches failed to solve the mystery and a rumour spread that she was haunted. When the ship was broken up in 1888, the skeleton of a riveter was found in her bilge, with a hammer beside him.

GETTING THERE NO 5 - THE BICYCLE

The first bicycles were called 'boneshakers' because they had hard tyres and seats. From 1839 (with Kirkpatrick Macmillan's design) to 1885 (with John Starley's Safety Bicycle), bikes gradually improved.

In 1872 a strange and rather dangerous contraption known as the 'penny-farthing' became popular. The huge front wheel was almost six feet from top to bottom and the seat was above the wheel. The penny-farthing was more of a bone-breaker than a bone-shaker. It went at quite a speed once you got going.

The Safety Bicycle appeared in 1885. It had a low seat and equal-sized wheels and women liked it, although they had trouble wearing long skirts over a cross-bar.

GETTING THERE NO 6 – THE HORSELESS CARRIAGE

The first cars came later. They looked like carriages, without the horses. In 1885, the Germans Karl Benz and Gottlieb Daimler invented the first workable petrol-driven motorcar. Meanwhile an Austrian diplomat called Emil Jellinek had secured the selling rights on a large number of Daimler cars which he sold under the name Mercedes, after his daughter Mercedes Jellinek. In 1925 he joined forces with Karl Benz, and the cars made by the new company were called Mercedes-Benz cars.

WORKSHOP OF THE WORLD

DARK SATANIC MILLS

By the time of the Great Exhibition, Britain was known as the 'Workshop of the World'. Britain was years ahead of her competitors when it came to making and selling things. This was because of Britain's no.1 invention – the Industrial Revolution. Until the Industrial Revolution most things could take ages to make, by hand or on simple machines. This is how the Industrial Revolution worked:

☞ FACTORIES AND MACHINES. Inventors thought up machines which were housed in factories. A steam engine with the strength of 880 men could work 50,000 textile spinning spindles. This machine needed only 750 workers to make as much yarn as 200,000 men had done by hand.

☞ LOTS OF WORKERS. Hundreds of thousands of farmworkers had no jobs on the land because of more efficient farming techniques. They migrated to the crowded cities where factories were booming.

☞ LOTS OF PEOPLE TO BUY THINGS. Britain's population bomb had exploded. By 1901 there were 17 million more people than in 1830. They all needed shoes, beds, towels, shirts, plates, knives and forks. There were millions and millions more people in the British Empire. (See page 94.)

☞ INVESTMENT. Some of the profits were ploughed back into new machines to make things more quickly in new factories.

DARK SATANIC MILLS

Factories spread like a plague. They came in all shapes and sizes, large ironworks in South Wales, small cutlery workshops in Sheffield, candle factories in Cheshire, choking potteries in Staffordshire. The mills of Yorkshire and Lancashire were housed in huge buildings six and more storeys high, with hundreds of windows.

FACTORY FODDER

Who made all the goods in Victoria's time?

Factories sucked people into their black greedy jaws. Employers needed people to keep the machines turning and children were the cheapest to employ. Children as young as four years old were employed to clear out waste material from under the dangerous, fast-moving machines. Women came next. Their labour was pretty cheap, as they were often desparate for money to feed their children. Men were paid the most.

In many families, the parents could not get factory work and children were the breadwinners. Both adults and children worked long hours and often fell asleep at their machines, with horrible results.

 Throughout the British dominions slaves were free by 1833, when slavery was finally abolished.

FACTORY ACTS

The Earl of Shaftesbury led the campaign to improve working conditions for women and children. During the nineteenth century there was a slow process of reform, bringing in better working conditions. A number of acts were passed in parliament.

1819: No children under nine could work in cotton mills. Those under sixteen were only allowed to work twelve hours a day.

1833: Children aged nine to thirteen to only work forty-eight hours a week. Government inspectors were appointed to check on the factories. Part-time education to be provided for factory chldren.

1844. Women to work only twelve hours a day, children aged eight to thirteen, six and a half hours.

In spite of these reforms conditions continued to be harsh for many people. The Chartists were workers who demanded better conditions from the government. Fear of uprisings made reform more likely.

OLD KING COAL

If you think that working in a Victorian factory was bad, digging coal was absolutely dreadful. To produce the steam for the machines, factories needed lots of coal.

The coal was largely hand-dug by soot-blackened men with picks and shovels. Women and children dragged the coal along the shafts and tunnels which were narrow and low. Children, being small, were just right for the job. The women and children were sometimes chained and belted like dogs in a cart. They appeared 'black, saturated with sweat and more than half-naked, crawling upon their hands and feet, and dragging their loads behind them'.

Other work moving coal on the surface was also done by women.

Women carried the coal from the tunnels to the surface up ladders, in baskets on their heads. The coal was often so heavy that it took two men to lift a basket onto a woman's head.

In 1842, a law was passed to stop children under ten from working in coal mines.

Booming Cities

Build 'em Fast, Build 'em Cheap

A modern town has sewers, street lights, a water supply and electricity. But in Victorian times, cheap houses were put up anywhere that a space could be found.

Factories burned coal for power. Houses burned coal for heat. Coal made lots of thick choking smoke which blackened houses and poisoned the atmosphere.

Buildings were often put up before water and sewage pipes were laid down so a single tap or pump might have to serve hundreds of people. Toilet waste was carried away by 'nightsoil men'. Some seeped into the water supply and rivers became polluted by factory and human waste. In 1858, the Thames in London became so smelly that the year was known as 'the year of the Great Stink'!

These are some of the things you might find in a Victorian city:

The cheap houses were badly built, cold and damp. In Whitechapel, London, as many as forty people could have been found living in a tiny terraced house, with ten, or more, people to a single room.

Unable to find rooms, many lived in cellars, under bridges, or even in sewers. Homeless people or drunks out on the street could hire a 'penny hang'. This was a space on a thick rope. There was no room to lie down. You hung across it.

The new cities were filled with rubbish. In 1833, when a courtyard in Leeds was cleared out, seventy-five cartloads of filth were taken away. People did not yet realise the importance of cleanliness.

GEORGE SMITH

"In 1838, when I was a child of about seven years, I was employed by a relative to assist him in making bricks. He thought kicks and blows formed the best means of obtaining the maximum of work from a lad; as if that weren't enough, excessively long hours of work were added.

At nine years of age my employment consisted in continually carrying about forty pounds of clay upon my head, from the clay heap on the table to where the bricks were made. This labour had to be performed, almost without intermission, for thirteen hours daily. Sometimes my labours were increased by my having to work all night at the kitchen.

One time I had a massive task to do. After my usual day's work, I had to carry 1,200 nine-inch bricks from the brick-maker to the floors on which they were laid to harden. I walked at least fourteen miles that night, backwards and forwards. For seven of those miles I was carrying 5 kilos of clay in my arms, (delivering the load). This was as well as lifting the clay and carrying it some distance to the maker, in the first place. I shifted 5½ tonnes in all. For six pence! After this enormous effort I was so tired that I became ill and couldn't work again for several weeks."

THE WORKHOUSE

If you didn't have any legal way of earning money you could end up in a workhouse. To poor people fear of the workhouse was almost worse than fear of death. Those too old, too young or too sick to work, or just unable to find a job, were put there.

Some bad things about workhouses:

- Families were split up. Men and women, boys and girls were separated.

- Work was hard. It included - washing clothes, picking ropes apart, crushing animal bones for fertilizer.

- Food was terrible. The men at Andover workhouse ate the rotting meat from the bones they were given to crush. Yuk!

- You were unlikely to get out again.

In Victorian times, workhouses were made deliberately harsh, to discourage people from being unemployed.

WHAT DID VICTORIA THINK?

Victoria felt sorry for poor people, but what could she do? On the one hand, she knew that their unhappy lives weren't all their own fault. But on the other hand, if God hadn't intended poor people to do all the hard work, he wouldn't have invented them, wouldn't he? After all where would things be without them?

You can't argue with God! So, like most rich people throughout history, Victoria thought it was best to leave things the way they were, with the rich at the top and the poor at the bottom – very convenient really.

VICIOUS VILLAINS

CRIME IN THE GRIME

Early in Victoria's reign, things were tough for villains. Some were transported to Australia, such as happened to William Pearson, after he'd committed lots of crimes in England. I made a copy of his crime-sheet, which I had to sneak out of the court. It's over the page.

A convict ship off to Australia

CRIME SHEET

NAME WILLIAM PEARSON
AGE 12
NATIVE PLACE NOTTINGHAM
HEIGHT 4 FT 8 INS
HAIR DARK BROWN
LATEST CHARGE STEALING KNIVES

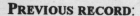

PREVIOUS RECORD:

CRIME	PUNISHMENT/ TIME LOCKED UP
STEALING KNIVES	1 month
STEALING BREAD	7 days
VAGRANCY	2 months 14 days
STEALING MONEY	6 months
STEALING MONEY	4 months
STEALING FRUIT	3 days & flogged
STEALING FRUIT	whipped
STEALING HAM	flogged
STEALING RAZORS	3 months
STEALING APPLES	1 month
FIGHTING	7 days
STEALING MONEY	1 month
STEALING EGGS	flogged
STEALING FOOD	2 months
ROBBING SHOP	3 months
STEALING HATS	2 months
STEALING FOWLS	3 months

VILLAINS

Victorian villains could be pretty nasty. Here are four extra-nasty ones that Victoria would have read about in the papers.

JACK THE RIPPER

The most gruesome of all was Jack the Ripper. The trouble is, we don't know much about him. All we know is that he killed at least five women in the East End of London. His reign of terror lasted for a period of three months in 1888.

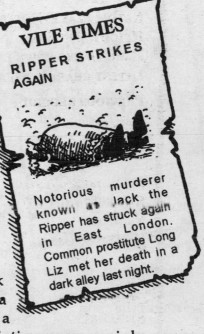

VILE TIMES

RIPPER STRIKES AGAIN

Notorious murderer known as Jack the Ripper has struck again in East London. Common prostitute Long Liz met her death in a dark alley last night.

The few people who think they saw him say he was a tall, slim, pale man with a black moustache. His victims were mainly poor prostitutes and he attacked them with a knife.

The unlucky victims were Martha Turner, Mary Ann Nicholls (Pretty Polly), Anne Chapman (Dark Annie), Elizabeth Stride (Long Liz), Catherine Eddowes and Mary Kelly. There are many theories about who did it. Some thought it might have been Victoria's grandson, the Duke of Clarence.

VILE TIMES

PRISONER HUNG AT LAST

Evil poisoner Mary Ann Cotton was hung yesterday. She had murdered at least ten people, including five husbands.

In 1852, twenty-year-old Mary Ann Cotton married a labourer called William Mowbray and moved to Devon, where she had five children. Four died young. They moved to the north-east where Mary Ann took a job as a nurse. She had three more children, who all died. Then her husband died.

In 1866, she married again, an engineer called George Wood, who died fourteen months later. And so it went on, through five marriages. One day, Mary Ann went to visit her mother because she thought her mother 'might die soon' – she did, nine days later.

All in all, twenty-one of her relations and acquaintances died, mostly of stomach troubles. It turned out she had been spreading arsenic around their beds. She was caught after she asked a social worker to take a stepson off her hands. When the child died a few days later, the social worker grew suspicious. She was brought to trial. The case shocked Victorian England. Mary Ann Cotton was hanged at Durham in 1873.

CHARLIE PEACE

Charlie Peace was a small man with a limp and a hook arm. He could play the violin well and was very strong and determined. For twenty years he lived as a cat burglar without once getting caught, carrying his tools in a violin case. He carried on an affair with a neighbour's wife, Katherine Dyson, in Sheffield. When her huge husband got angry and chased Peace down an alleyway, Peace shot him dead.

VILE TIMES

MURDERER FOUND IN SNOW

Arch-crook Charlie Peace was found unconscious in the snow yesterday, having jumped from the train taking him to justice in Sheffield.

Peace and his family moved to London, where he became a respectable churchgoer, all the while continuing to burgle houses. His wife and son lived in the basement, while Peace and his mistress lived on the floor above as Mr and Mrs Thompson.

Peace was finally caught raiding a London house. He shot a policeman while trying to escape but was captured and went on trial – under the name of Ward. He got life imprisonment. Then his mistress revealed his real name in order to get the £100 reward for the Sheffield murder. When he was being taken back to Sheffield by the police, Peace jumped out of the train but fell badly and was recaptured. At his trial Peace confessed to more murders. He was hanged on February 25th, 1879.

VILE TIMES

BABIES' BODIES FOUND IN THAMES

Another parcel containing the remains of a small baby was found yesterday in the River Thames. Police have found an address on the brown wrapping paper.

AMELIA DYER

Amelia Dyer was broke, so she began to earn a living as a baby farmer in Bristol. She simply advertised for children that needed looking after.

After a spell in prison, she moved to Caversham, near Reading, and changed her name and way of working. She murdered the children, and so saved herself the cost and trouble of looking after them.

One day, bargemen working on the River Thames, near Reading, discovered a parcel and a bag, and later other parcels, all containing small bodies. Amelia Dyer was contacted because one victim was wrapped in brown paper on which her address could still be read.

At her trial, Amelia's daughter Polly told how one day her mother had come to visit her holding a baby girl, Doris Marmon. When Polly came back from fetching some coal, the baby had disappeared and her mother was pushing a battered old carpet bag under the sofa. Amelia Dyer was hanged in 1896, leaving a note to clear her daughter which said, "What was done I did myself."

DEVILISH DICTIONARY

There were all kinds of small-time criminals, and in London they had special names. Here are some of the main ones.

BEAK HUNTER
Stole poultry

BLOBBER
Begged with
hard-luck stories

BUG HUNTER
Robbed drunks

CRACKSMAN
Safe-breaker

BROADSMAN
Card-sharp

BIT FAKER
Forged coins

DRAUGHTSMAN
Stole from carriages

FLIMP
Purse-snatcher

JUDY
Woman,
prostitute

LAG
Convict

OTHERS INCLUDED:

BEARER UP	Bully-thief with woman helping
BLUDGER	Footpad, mugger
BUZZER	Thief, pickpocket
CASH CARRIER	Pimp, ponce
DUFFER	Cheating street-seller
FINE-WIRER	Skilled pickpocket
GONOPH	Crude pickpocket
KIDSMAN	Ran child thieves
MOOCHER	Vagrant
PALMER	Shoplifter
SCREEVER	Forger of papers
SNAKESMAN	Thin boy burglar
SNOOZER	Hotel thief

MUTTON CHOPS AND CRINOLINES

ROYAL FRUMP

Victoria had no taste in dress. She would not have made today's fashion pages. On a visit to Paris in 1855, it was noted how dowdy she looked. Parisians were amazed by her enormous handbag, decorated with a portrait of a poodle, and her gown, embroidered in geraniums, which looked like 'a seed catalogue'.

Only the rich could dress in a grand Victorian way. Clothes were expensive. There were no decent sewing machines and clothes were made by hand.

Factory workers had no chance of keeping their clothes clean in all the smoke and dirt. Every piece of clothing had to last as long as possible. The older and more patched it was, the shabbier it became. The children of workers wore clothes that had been passed down two or three times, and many went barefoot.

WOMEN WEARING HUGE SKIRTS

Imagine getting dressed and needing a crane to help put your clothes on! It was almost like that for many wealthy women in the first half of Victoria's reign.

The fashion was for huge skirts, worn with layers of petticoats underneath to help fill them out. As the skirts got wider and bigger, they became too heavy to

wear, and so crinolines were invented. They were like cages – hoops of bamboo, whalebone or steel which fastened to the wearer's waist. Petticoats and dresses were then put over the top and rested on the cage. Dresses like these were enormous, so big that women got stuck in doorways and turnstiles.

SLIM WAISTS

Another fashion was for horribly slim waists. In order to look like an hourglass, women were laced so tightly into whalebone corsets that they could hardly breathe, and kept fainting.

Some women even had their bottom ribs removed to make them slimmer. The ideal waist for a young woman was about eighteen inches, so that her husband might just reach right round with both hands.

MRS BLOOMER

In 1851 an American called Mrs Amelia Bloomer introduced 'rational dress', which consisted of long frilly trousers tied at the ankles, called 'pantalettes'. This sort of clothing was much more comfortable and healthier for women.

Her supporters held meetings in London, wearing the new clothes which were at once nicknamed 'bloomers'. They were jeered at when they walked the streets.

To the Victorians the idea of women in trousers ("trying to look like men") was shocking. Mrs Bloomer was accused of trying to wreck marriages. Her rational dress never caught on.

It wasn't until the next century, that women were to dare to ask for more independence – in dress, in jobs and in personal freedom.

If you want to get ahead get a hat

No Victorian would be seen dead without a hat. Manchester factory workers who could not afford a cap wore hats made out of paper bags.

The hat you wore told others where you stood in the social pecking order. Upper-class men wore shiny top hats. For evening wear they might wear an 'opera hat' which collapsed so it could be put underneath a theatre seat.

Working men wore soft, flat cloth-caps. If they couldn't afford a new one, they might buy one made from old clothes.

Piccadilly weepers

Beards became popular in the 1850s. The fashion began in the Crimean War when officers weren't able to shave, because of the lack of facilities. It quickly spread to civilians at home. Beards made men look older. It helped a young man look solid and dependable to his elders. Long side-whiskers, known as 'Piccadilly weepers', replaced beards as fashion accessories until the 1870s.

MASHERS AND HEAVY SWELLS

In about 1860 'mashers' and 'heavy swells' appeared. They wore trousers patterned with enormous squares of black and brown, short bright jackets, and green or yellow waistcoats.

They sported bunches of flowers in their button holes, huge floppy bow-ties, yellow boots and stovepipe hats. At night, they added a full opera cloak.

It cost a fortune. Fortunately, the fashion vanished in the 1870s.

PETTICOATS AND SAILOR SUITS

Throughout most of the Victorian era, rich girls and boys in the nursery were dressed alike up to the age of four or even older. It was common to see infant boys wearing bonnet, dress and petticoats.

Then at the age of four or five or six, the Victorian male was 'breeched'. He was taken out of dresses and put into breeches or trousers.

Sailor suits were the favourite, but towards the end of the 1800s, he might breech into a hunting suit of Norfolk jacket and knickerbockers: a miniature version of adult clothes. Dressed like that, he looked like a midget adult.

The most horrid thing to wear was the 'Little Lord Fauntleroy' velvet knickerbocker suit with lace collar. The suit was popular for wealthier children, but some adults wore it – for example the playwright and novelist Oscar Wilde wore one sometimes. It made the wearer look like a pampered poodle.

FIVE THINGS YOU MIGHT NOT KNOW ABOUT VICTORIAN CLOTHES

1. PURPLE RAGE. In 1856 W. H. Perkin discovered that a strong dye could be made from coal-tar. Perkin's new dye was bright purple. In no time at all purple became all the rage. Gowns, gloves, feathers, hat, ribbons, all were purple. One writer declared, 'we shall soon have purple omnibuses and purple houses'.

2. LEG OF MUTTON. This wasn't what sheep stood on, but a fashion for fat sleeves on dresses during the 1890s.

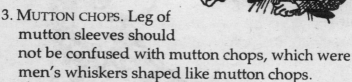

3. MUTTON CHOPS. Leg of mutton sleeves should not be confused with mutton chops, which were men's whiskers shaped like mutton chops.

4. HAND-ME-DOWN. Hand-me-down clothes were not second hand. They were ready-made clothes which the shopkeeper took down from the high drawers in his shop. The term was used by rich people who could afford hand-made clothes.

5. OLD-CLOTHES MEN. Working people might buy their clothes second-hand from market stalls or from 'old-clothes men' who peddled their wares around city streets. The clothes were often dirty and a source of disease. The French, who never bought rags no matter how poor they were, thought the English disgusting.

GOODBYE ALBERT

THE BIRTH OF GLOOM

Poor Victoria. Lovely handsome Prince Albert passed away on 14th December 1861. He died of typhoid, probably caused by the bad drains at Windsor. Victoria blamed it all on stress caused by the behaviour of their son, Bertie, who had lots of girlfriends.

Victoria gave up on life when Albert died. She wanted nothing more than to die herself and join him. She buried him in a mausoleum on the Windsor Castle estate, beneath a white marble statue. She also had a statue made for herself, ready for her own death. She looked at it every time she visited Albert's tomb (twice a year: on his birthday and at Christmas). She couldn't wait to join him.

PROBLEM: Victoria was only 44 years old. It was to be another forty years before her statue could be dusted down.

SOLUTION: Make everybody's life a misery. Grief became a habit for her, and for many of her subjects. Many of them wished she would hurry up and join her husband.

PAINT IT BLACK

Victoria went into mourning, which was fair enough. Most widows wore black, often for a year. But Victoria wanted the whole country to join her, and she was not seen in public for two years.

Victoria wore black, loads of it. The royal staff wore black. The Queen's ministers wore black. The royal horses wore black. There were shops in London which sold nothing but black; ostrich feathers for women's hats, sashed crepe 'weepers' (crepe bands) for men's tall hats, black plumes for horses. Even jewellery was supposed to be black, and jet became popular.

The servants were not allowed to smile or be seen to have fun. Life at Windsor, Balmoral, Buckingham Palace and Osborne was a grind of deadly gloom.

After two years Victoria allowed her women servants to wear other colours, but they had to wear black armbands when on duty until 1869. Eight years in mourning is a long time by any standard.

THE INVISIBLE QUEEN

Victoria became a hermit. She refused to make public appearances for years, and eventually the government and the newspapers started to complain. 'Why are we paying her all this money when she does nothing to earn it?' they asked. She became known as the 'Royal Malingerer'.

The Prime Minister told her to buck up, but she took no notice. The only thing she liked doing was going on holiday – she went to France or Italy for a few weeks every year, not to mention a couple of months in Scotland.

She wanted lots of statues of Albert to be made and she tried to persuade other people to pay for them. The trouble was that nobody else loved Albert like she did.

After Wolverhampton became the first town to erect a statue of Albert, in November 1866, Victoria hit on a plan. She went off like a shot to unveil it and while she was there she surprised everyone by knighting the mayor, John Morris. The message was clear: put up a statue to dear Albert and, hey presto, you're a Sir! Suddenly statues of Albert sprang up all over the place.

ALBERT MEMORIAL

Finally a massive, expensive memorial statue to Albert was put up in Hyde Park, near to where the Great Exhibition had been. He is still there today, seated under a huge canopy, reading the Exhibition catalogue. The memorial has seven levels:

CONTINENTS	Europe, America, Asia, Africa
INDUSTRY	Agriculture, Manufacturing, Commerce, Engineering
ARTS	169 relief sculptures of poets, painters, architects and musicians
ALBERT	Reading the Catalogue
KNOWLEDGE	Astronomy, Chemistry, Geology, Geometry, Rhetoric, Medicine, Philosophy, Physiology
MORALITY	Faith, Hope, Charity and others
RELIGION	Angels

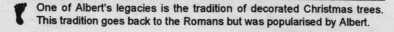
One of Albert's legacies is the tradition of decorated Christmas trees. This tradition goes back to the Romans but was popularised by Albert.

Later, all sorts of grand buildings were built in a long line running from the Albert Memorial. These include the Albert Hall, the Victoria and Albert Museum and the Science Museum.

LEAVE IT ALONE

Albert's clothes were laid out every day. A tinted deathbed photograph hung over the royal bed, on the side on which he had slept. Towels were changed every day and Albert's unused chamber pot was scrubbed and scoured.

Visitors to the royal palaces had to sign two visitors' books: one Victoria's and the other Albert's. They were calling on a dead man! Victoria even carried around a small portrait of Albert in a jewelled frame. Whenever she visited anywhere she held up the photo so that Albert might have a good look too!

VICTORIA'S OTHER MEN

Victoria always liked to have a man she could turn to. When she was young, there was Uncle Leopold. When she became Queen, there was Prime Minister Melbourne. Then of course, there was dear Albert. But who could she turn to now?

She picked a bad-tempered, whisky-drinking, heavy-smoking Scot called John Brown. He had been Albert's favourite gillie on their visits to Scotland. On Albert's death, Victoria brought Brown to Windsor. She commanded that he was to be known as 'The Queen's Highland Servant'. This special title meant that Brown could get away with murder. Though Victoria detested the smell of tobacco, Brown smoked his awful pipe in her presence.

Brown liked a drink a two and he often smelt like a distillery. Once at Balmoral, Victoria waited in her carriage in vain for Brown to come and drive. Finally her secretary found him drunk on his bed. Brown staggered downstairs and, without a word to Victoria, pulled himself aboard and off they set. She was often drunk too, so it was said, although this may have been because her servants finished off the whisky bottles for her.

Brown could be very rude. He once stopped the Prime Minister in mid-speech by telling him to his face "Ye've said enough!"

In the Scottish highlands, a gillie is a gentleman's servant.

Top people didn't like Brown. He was rough, Scottish and wore a kilt. He spoke to the queen as if she were just a normal human being, which Victoria loved, but the top people didn't.

Whispered rumours said that there "was something going on" between Victoria and Brown. After all, she was only forty-four and he was just five years younger. Some newspapers called her Mrs Brown, as they had called her Mrs Melbourne some years before. They poked fun at Brown's bare knees.

Brown was rude to servants and courtiers alike. He was often drunk. The gillies' ball at Balmoral was always a drunken knees-up. Victoria joined in with the odd dram of whisky and Scottish country dance.

In 1883, Brown died after twenty years of service, with never a day off. Victoria ordered that his room at Windsor be left undisturbed, apart from a fresh flower that was to be placed on his pillow each morning. She also ordered a statue of him to be put up at Balmoral.

Victoria became miserable again. She wanted to hide away. Her carriage windows were covered with blinds. When she travelled to Scotland, the public was kept from station platforms when her train passed. She sank into a deeper gloom than ever.

BREAD AND DRIPPING

MORE SOUP, OLIVER?

Apart from John Brown, Victoria loved other Scottish things, especially haggis. This was not a Scottish gamekeeper but a delicacy made of the heart, lungs and liver of a sheep, chopped up with suet, onions and porridge, and boiled in a sheep's stomach-bag.

Because of gout 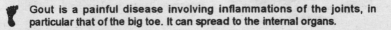, Victoria was forbidden to drink wine. She drank only whisky and water at her meals and had whisky instead of milk in her tea. Victoria even had her own whisky specially distilled for her near Balmoral, at the small distillery of John Begg.

The first slimming diet was published in 1862. Obviously Victoria didn't read it. In her fifties she weighed over twelve stone (76.4 kilos). She was almost as wide as she was tall.

Gout is a painful disease involving inflammations of the joints, in particular that of the big toe. It can spread to the internal organs.

VICTORIAN FACTS ABOUT FOOD AND DRINK

In rich houses, an army of cooks and servants prepared and served enormous amounts of food. Ham, tongue, pheasant, kedgeree (a rice and fish dish), kippers, eggs, bacon, kidneys, porridge and a choice of teas might be served for breakfast alone.

Moustache cups, with a special curved ledge, were designed to lift whiskers clear when drinking tea or coffee.

During the 1880s many brand names began to appear which are still with us today. Among them are Cadbury's chocolate, OK sauce, Bovril, Peak Frean biscuits and Sainsbury food stores.

According to the French philosopher Hippolyte Taine, writing in the 1860s, an average English gentleman ate four sheep a year.

In the days before refrigerated transport, dairy cows were kept in the middle of cities to provide fresh milk. Such a cow started the great fire of Chicago in 1871, by knocking over a lantern in the straw.

Tinned food became popular after an easy-to-use tin opener was invented in 1866.

A VICTORIAN CAKE RECIPE

Here's a Victorian cake recipe for you to try:

QUEEN'S FINGERS

You will need:

FOR CAKE

4-5oz (140 grammes)	butter or margarine
2½ oz (70 grammes)	castor sugar
4 oz (115 grammes)	plain flour, sifted
4 oz (115 grammes)	ground rice or semolina
1 oz (30 grammes)	ground almonds
A few drops	almond essence
Plenty of	jam

FOR ICING

4 oz (115 grammes)	icing sugar
A few drops	lemon juice
A tablespoon of	warm water

Mix the butter and castor sugar thoroughly. Add the rice, or semolina, the flour, the ground almonds and almond essence. Knead until it makes a nice stiff paste, then roll out into a big slab. Cut this slab into three equal pieces. Sandwich them together with lots of lovely jam. Place on a baking tray and shove into a pre-heated oven at gas mark 5 (190° C) for twenty minutes. Remember to use oven gloves as the oven will be hot.

Make the icing by mixing together the icing sugar, warm water, and the lemon juice. When the cake is cooked spread the icing over the top, cut into finger shapes – and gobble up.

CRUEL GRUEL

While Victoria and other rich people were dining on the best delicacies that money could buy, the food of poor people was very different. The very poor in the workhouse ate a coarse porridge called gruel. It was roughly made of ground oatmeal, served thinly. Those unwilling to go to the workhouse for such a miserable dinner could always raid the pig troughs, which many of them did.

Workers living ten to a room and forty to a house often did not have a kitchen or a stove to cook on. Even if they could afford meat, how could they cook it? So they took their meat, when they could get it, to a bake-house, where for a small fee it was cooked for them and they picked it up after work. Another way to get hot food and cups of tea was to buy it at market stalls. The streets were full of hot potato sellers and roast chestnut men.

From the 1860s onwards, it became possible to buy freshly fried fish and chips in most industrial towns, because the new railways could bring fresh fish packed in ice. Chips were a French invention.

This is why they are called 'French fries' in the United States.

In the 1880s food became cheaper. Refrigerated ships brought meat from America and New Zealand. Cheaper wheat was shipped in from the United States and Argentina. The railways and improved roads made it less expensive to transport food, so things got a little better.

Farm workers were worse paid than factory workers, but they had other benefits; they had a bit of land, if only a garden, to grow vegetables, there was often the farmer's crops to slip into a pocket, and a snared rabbit, poached pheasant or fish to fill the cookpot.

Factory owners often paid their workers in tokens which could only be spent at the factory shop, where the price of food was kept high. In 1844 a group of weavers in Rochdale, Lancashire, each put in a pound and bought food to stock a shop of their own. They sold goods at market prices but gave back a share of the profits to their customers. This was the first Co-operative or Co-op shop.

BREAD LINE

For many years bread cost more than it should have done. This was because farmers kept the price of corn high so as to give themselves a fatter profit. Through their friends in Parliament who made the laws, they made sure that foreign corn, which would have been cheaper than British, was heavily taxed.

The rich looked down on margarine when it was invented in the 1870s. They could afford to as they had never gone short of butter. Everyone else greeted margarine with delight. At last there was something other than dripping to go with their bread. White bread and jam became very popular and jam factories sprang up all over the place.

When the craze for white bread started, some rascally bakers added stuff like plaster to their flour. This caused a lot of anger in the early 1840s – a time of great hunger. During the 'Hungry Forties', many British and Irish people emigrated to the United States. They often died of illness on appalling sea journeys.

Dripping is fat left over from cooking meat.

SLIPPERY OYSTERS FACT

Today, oysters are an expensive treat. In Victorian days, they were cheap and plentiful. It was not unusual for a gentleman to slurp his way through sixty of the slithery, sloppy things.

THE GREAT IRISH FAMINE

In 1845 Ireland was a country of about eight million people. About half of them depended on growing potatoes for their food. In that year a strange disease struck the Irish potato crop, leaving millions hungry.

 The next year, 1846, the potato plants went black and withered to the ground overnight.

That winter was bitterly cold, and many people were left homeless, hungry, starving and freezing. The 1847 crop was also disastrous. It is thought that one and a half million Irish people died as a result of the famine, and the same number emigrated.

TRUE TALES:

SHIPWRECK

Emigration to another country was one way of escaping poverty at home, but it could be a dangerous business. A boy called Walters was one of eleven boys who were sent to America.

Their ship left Liverpool on the 23rd August 1853. Twelve days out, there was a storm and they were blown towards a reef of rocks. The ship was grounded and then was struck by an enormous wave which smashed it up.

In the boys' cabin, the water rose to their waists. Walters climbed on a table which floated up to a skylight, where he could see that the ship had broken into three pieces. One of the boys was trapped and called out for twenty minutes, but no one could find or free him. Many were maimed by lumps of broken wood floating about. They were stuck inside for seven hours, with the water rising, before the ship broke up around them.

Nine of the eleven boys died, among 287 who died out of 351 passengers. It turned out they had been wrecked on the Scottish Isle of Barra. The survivors were rescued by islanders, taken to the island of Skye, and then to hospital in Glasgow. Walters, pitifully thin, went back to London and wrote his story – but he still wanted to emigrate, this time to Australia!

GIZZA JOB!

SCRAPING A LIVING

Victoria had hundreds of servants. All rich Victorians kept lots of them. Here are some typical servant jobs:

SERVANT JOBS

MEN

BUTLER	in charge of the others
FOOTMAN	shoes, door, odd jobs
COACHMAN	drive horses
GROOM	look after horses
GARDENER	garden!
VALET	dress the gentleman

WOMEN

COOK	look after food
KITCHEN MAID	help cook
LAUNDRYWOMAN	cleans clothes
CHAMBERMAID	clean the bedrooms
LADY'S MAID	dress the lady
NURSEMAID	look after babies

MAID OF ALL WORK

An average middle class family would have a Maid-of-all-Work. It sounds tough, and it was. She was expected to do everything. This was her typical day:

BEFORE BREAKFAST

Get up at 6 am. Polish all the metalwork. Brush out the flues (chimneys) and light the kitchen range. Put on kettle and polish knives and boots as the kettle boils. Clean and sweep the breakfast parlour. Sweep the hall and whiten the doorstep, then light the drawing room fire. Collect and sift the cinders, Change into clean clothes. Dust the breakfast room and lay the table. Serve the family breakfast.

AFTER BREAKFAST

Grab some breakfast for yourself in the kitchen. Clean bedrooms and empty chamberpots. Wash up everything in the kitchen. The lady of the house or her daughter may dust the ornaments, in case the maid breaks such precious things. Answer the door to tradesmen.

EVENING

Cook and serve the main meal of the day. Do a bit of washing up. Wait upon the lady of the family in the evening. Repair and make your own clothes. If it's Saturday, soak the white linens. If it's Monday, do the big clothes wash. Once a week, you might get an evening off.

STREET TRADERS

At least servants had a roof over their heads and a steady job. Life could be even tougher out on the streets. Here are some typical Victorian street jobs.

SCAVENGERS

Picked up anything they could get, especially from the River Thames at low tide. They would often walk into the sewers, looking for things they could sell again, like lead, iron or bottles. They could be attacked by fierce rats.

DREDGERMEN

Tried to find things in the river itself and might do a bit of smuggling or carrying in their rowing boats. Sometimes they were paid to fish out dead bodies from the river.

MUDLARKS
Small boys and old
women who picked up
coal from the river mud
and sold it.

DUST COLLECTORS
Quite well off. They had a horse and cart and took
rubbish to dustyards, where women sorted
everything into piles – dust (for manure or brick-
making), rags, bones, cinders and so on.

COSTERMONGERS
Sold fish, fruit and vegetables from barrows and
stalls. (They still do.) New or foreign foods, like nuts,
oranges and pineapples, did really well.
Costermongers were top of the street workers, and
had money to spend on a good time in the evenings.

OTHER TRADES
Ballad sellers, letter-writers, flower sellers, bird
catchers.

ANDREW CARNEGIE

A few of the Victorian poor rose to great heights, but it helped to go abroad, where there were more opportunities, and less prejudice against people from poor backgrounds.

Andrew Carnegie left Scotland in 1848 as a boy of thirteen with his parents, and sailed to America in an old whaling ship of 800 tons, the Wiscasset. *During the seven-week voyage he got to know the sailors, to help them and to learn from them.*

He was amazed by the bustle and excitement of New York and was thrilled when one of the sailors took him to a refreshment stand and bought him a sarsaparilla, (a tonic made from dried roots). He became a messenger boy, then a salesman, then a broker, then a railwayman. Finally he became owner of a huge iron and steel company that dominated United States industry, making full use of the cheap labour of all his fellow immigrants.

In 1901, the same year that Queen Victoria died, he sold out and spent the next eighteen years giving away 350 million dollars of his own money. It was a great American success story.

CAREERS ABROAD

During Victoria's reign, thousands of men, sometimes with their wives, sailed out from Britain to work in the countries of the British Empire. (See page 94.) Here are some of the things that they did:

SOLDIER

There was a great need for soldiers to defend and expand the Empire.

ENGINEER

Victorian engineers were in demand all over the world to build railways, bridges, mines and ships.

ADMINISTRATOR

There was work for people who could run the colonies, settle disputes, set up townships, and report back to Britain.

MISSIONARY

Christians – especially Protestants – felt it was very important to civilize the native peoples of the Empire and save their souls.

A MESS OF MINISTERS

DIZZY AND THE BOYS

Being a queen could be hard work. There were laws to sign, and governments to appoint, as well as buildings and other things to open. Victoria had to cope with politicians from two main political parties, the Whigs and the Tories.

TORIES
Tories tended to support the Queen and to dislike change. They were backed by ordinary landowners. Victoria was a bit of a Tory.

WHIGS
Whigs tended to oppose the Queen. They were led by powerful aristocrats and backed by tradesmen and manufacturers. Other name – Liberal Party.

ROYAL REPORT – PICK OF THE PRIME MINISTERS No 1 LORD MELBOURNE

PRIME MINISTER: 1834, 1835-41

PARTY: Whig (though a Tory at heart)

PRIME MINISTERIAL PROFILE: Charming, cultured, rather lazy. Liked to lounge about on sofas. His wife had a passionate affair with the poet Lord Byron, and he was named as the 'other man' in two divorce cases.

Melbourne was Prime Minister when Victoria came to the throne and they got on really well. He didn't help the workers much because he supported the Corn Laws, which kept the price of bread too high.

GENERAL: Melbourne was a pleasant enough Prime Minister, but his laziness and lack of care for the poor meant that he was not as effective as he should have been.

VERDICT: Could have tried harder.

PRIME MINISTER: 1834-35, 1841-46

PARTY: Tory, but a reforming one, almost a Whig.

PRIME MINISTERIAL PROFILE: Energetic, serious. Got on well with Prince Albert, but not Victoria.

Peel built up the modern Conservative party, and he had a lot of new ideas. He started the police force (nicknamed 'Peelers') and made other legal changes such as abolishing the Corn Laws and allowing Catholics to sit in Parliament. Under Peel the country grew richer.

GENERAL:
Peel
worked
hard and showed a flair for government. However his serious manner caused some problems.

VERDICT: Very efficient.

ROYAL REPORT
No 3 Benjamin Disraeli

PRIME MINISTER: 1868, 1874–80

PARTY: Tory

PRIME MINISTERIAL PROFILE: Clever, fancy dresser, liked jewelled rings, gaudy waistcoats, a goatee beard, and dyed hair. The son of a Spanish Jew. A successful novelist. Arranged for Victoria to become Empress of India. They got on well.

Disraeli led the Conservative Party in their struggles with Gladstone's Whig or Liberal Party. He doubled the number of people who could vote. He also brought in a Public Health Act and bought most of the Suez Canal for Britain. A keen Empire builder.

GENERAL: Disraeli was sometimes too clever for his own good. He was a popular politician but could get carried away. However he showed excellent leadership qualities and was a good team-worker.

VERDICT: Excellent.

Royal Report
No 4 William Gladstone

PRIME MINISTER: 1868-74, 1880-85, 1886, 1892-94

PARTY: Whig, though he started as a Tory.

PRIME MINISTERIAL PROFILE: High-minded and inspiring in public but could bore people in private. (He tended to talk as if making a speech.) Went out at night and talked to prostitutes, strictly out of concern for their welfare. Known as the Grand Old Man. He sat in Parliament for sixty-one years and was Prime Minister four times.

Gladstone spoke for the new industrial middle classes, and tried to cut taxes whenever he could. He

introduced many reforms and nearly got 'Home Rule' for Ireland. He opposed Disraeli's plans to build up the Empire.

GENERAL: Gladstone was honest and clever, but he could have lightened up a bit. His dreary speeches were annoying. He showed courage in standing up to the Empire builders.

VERDICT: Very trying, but meant well.

 Ireland was a British colony. The Irish wanted independence, or 'Home Rule'.

DIZZY OR GLADSTONE — WHO DID VICTORIA LIKE BEST?

No competition. Victoria complained that when Gladstone talked to her, he seemed to forget that he was not making a speech to Parliament. Having launched into his theme, Gladstone "mowed down his audience like a juggernaut".

Disraeli, on the other hand, was a good listener and was happy to talk about anything Victoria wanted to talk about. He flattered her.

One young lady sat next to both Disraeli and Gladstone at dinner parties on following nights. She said that after meeting Gladstone, she was convinced he was the cleverest man in England, but after meeting Disraeli, she was convinced that she was the cleverest woman in England.

MORE MINISTERS

There were plenty of other Prime Ministers around, though not all were interesting. Here they are:

Lord Russell (1846-52, 1865-66). Whig.

Earl of Derby (1852, 1858-9, 1866-8)
Tory (sometimes Whig!).

Lord Aberdeen (1852-55).
Somewhere in the middle.

Viscount Palmerston (1855-58, 1859-65).
Whig, Empire builder.

Marquis of Salisbury
(1885-86, 1886-92, 1895-1902).
Very Tory.

Earl of Rosebery (1894-95).
Another Whig. Empire builder.

The Jubilees

Prime ministers came and went, but Victoria, being Queen, kept her job. She didn't do it very well because she hid away from the public and wore black. She was not very popular. At last, in 1887, she came out of hiding – in a big way. By then she had been on the throne for fifty years. It was time for a Golden Jubilee party. Suddenly she found that she was more popular than she had ever been. Ten years later she had a Diamond Jubilee celebration.

And this is where we came in – a little fat lady dressed in black on a hot day with cheering crowds all around her.

Question

Collections were taken throughout the world for both Jubilees. What do you suppose Victoria wanted to spend the money on?

Answer

Right first time – another statue of Albert.

The shops filled up with souvenirs of the Jubilees. There were tea caddies and biscuit tins; tea pots in the shape of the queen's head with the lid a crown; walking sticks with the queen's head as the nob; and musical bustles  which played 'God Save the Queen' when the wearer sat down.

Poems were read, music composed, books written, hands shaken, crowds waved to, banquets eaten, drink swilled, bands paraded, portraits painted, statues unveiled and church bells rung.

Never was the monarchy more popular.

Bustles were padding which women wore beneath their skirts to make their bottoms look bigger.

WHERE THE SUN

AT LAST – THE BRITISH EMPIRE

All the time that Victoria was on the throne, Britain kept on getting richer and more powerful. Britain gradually gained power over other countries, and these countries together came to be called the British Empire. The Empire was huge. It stretched from Canada to Australia and from India to Africa. It was so big that the sun was always shining on some part

NEVER SETS

of it. On the maps, it used to be coloured red, so the map of the world looked as though someone had spilt a pot of red paint over it. At its greatest extent, a quarter of the world's population lived within its borders. Britain had never set out to have an empire as such, but it just grabbed opportunities for trade and raw materials, and tried to stop others grabbing them. The pieces of the Empire were called colonies. There were lots of them.

ONTROLLING POWER
VER LANDS OF THE
ORMER TURKISH
MPIRE.

STANLEY MEETS LIVINGSTONE

David Livingstone was a famous Scottish explorer and missionary. He set out in 1866 to find the source of the Nile. Nothing more was heard of him for several years. Was he lost?

American newspaper editor, Gordon Bennett, sent another explorer, Henry Morgan Stanley, to search for Livingstone. Stanley found him at Ujiji in East Africa in 1871. This is Stanley's description of the meeting:

"...as I advanced slowly towards him, I noticed he was pale, that he looked wearied and wan, that he had grey whiskers and a moustache, that he *wore a bluish cloth cap with a faded gold band on a red ground round it, and that he had on a red-sleeved waistcoat, and a pair of grey tweed trousers...*

*I took off my hat
and said:*

*'Dr. Livingstone, I
presume?'*

*'Yes,' said he, with
a kind, cordial smile, lifting his cap
slightly. I replaced my hat on my head,
and he replaced his cap, and we both
grasped hands. I then said aloud: 'I
thank God, doctor, I have been
permitted to see you.'*

*'I feel thankful that I am here to
welcome you.'"*

*Livingstone carried on looking for the
source of the Nile, and died in Africa
two years later.*

Check out my scrap-book of cuttings about the British Empire

New British citizens 1860

Britain abolished slavery in its own empire in 1833, but the trade has continued in America. Many runaway slaves have settled in Britain, often arriving as sailors. The first black communities are growing up around Cardiff and Liverpool. Trade with the Far East has also brought incomers from China, India and Malaya.

Empire News

CIRCULATION: 10 million

Oz strikes gold 1851

Gold has been discovered in Australia. Thousands of people are flooding in from all over the world in a rush for the gold. Many have come from America now that gold has run out in California, which had its own rush in 1849.

Dizzy buys Suez canal 1875

Disraeli, the British Prime Minister, has nipped in and bought a huge chunk of shares in the Suez Canal for Britain. He has borrowed the £4,000,000 price from a wealthy banker called Rothschild. The Suez Canal, which saves ships sailing all round Africa to India, was opened in 1869. Britain now has control of the fastest route to the East and India.

Irish leader dead
1891

Irish leader, Parnell, has died, having failed in his brave attempt to win self-government for Ireland, Britain's oldest colony. Parnell came close to his target by cashing in on strong anti-British feeling following the Irish famine. Parnell was recently the victim of dirty tricks, including a forged letter saying he supported the murder of two British politicians in Phoenix Park, Dublin. Parnell's love for married woman Kitty O'Shea has also unfairly blackened his name.

African carve up
1884

Europe has got together to carve up Africa. France, Germany, Belgium and Britain have decided to slice up the continent as if they were cutting a cake. Italy and Spain are also there for the crumbs. Nobody has told the Africans yet, but they'll soon find out.

White man's burden

Poet of the Empire, Rudyard Kipling, has called the Empire 'the White Man's Burden'. It costs money to keep colonies. Armies are needed to keep trouble at bay. Governors and civil servants are needed to run the countries. Taxes have to be collected. Railways have to be built.

British Empire ending
1901

Britain's colonies are following the lead of New Zealand and Canada, and breaking away from the British Empire. Soon the British Empire may be replaced by the British Commonwealth, a group of self-governing states still keeping the British monarch as their head.

SOME YOU WIN...

In January 1879, a British army invaded
Zululand in South Africa. It was a mistake. The
Zulus were proud and fierce warriors, as the
Brits soon discovered. 1500 soldiers, even with
rifles and automatic 'Gatling guns' (huge
machine guns on wheels), were no match for
the spears and clubs of 20,000 Zulus. The
British were massacred at Isandhlwana.
Shortly afterwards, two hundred surviving
soldiers held off an army of 4000 Zulus at a
mission hospital at Rorke's Drift. The British
fired over 20,000 bullets during the fight. After
the battle, eleven Victoria Cross medals were
awarded for bravery – a record for one battle.
Rorke's Drift showed that in the long run
spears and clubs were no match for modern
weapons. In July 1879, the British army
overran the Zulu capital, Ulundi, and captured
Cetewayo, King of the Zulus.

Empire builders wanted South Africa because
it had farmland, gold and diamonds, and
because they had designs on some of Africa
further north.

JEWEL IN THE CROWN

Victoria always wanted to go to India but feared the heat would make her ill. Instead, she had a special room built by an Indian architect which she filled with carpets, tiger skins and other Indian things. It was called the Durbar Room

The Victorians thought India was Britain's number one colony. India was the 'jewel in the crown', and the massive Indian Koor-i-Noor diamond was added to the royal crown when Victoria was made Empress of India in 1867. It was a huge country. It seems amazing that a handful of British administrators and soldiers could rule a land of 300 million people – but they did!

THE MUNSHI

Victoria took on a 24-year-old servant called Abdul Karim to work in the Durbar Room, but he soon let it be known that being a servant was beneath him. He was a Munshi (a clerk), an important person. Victoria asked him to teach her the Hindustani language.

The Palace officials loathed the Munshi. He went everywhere with the Queen. He kept inviting friends and relations to stay. He was almost as close to her as John Brown had been.

A durbar was the court of an Indian ruler

EMPIRE THINGS NAMED
AFTER VICTORIA AND ALBERT

LAKE VICTORIA. Africa's largest lake. The second biggest freshwater lake in the world. Named by British explorer John Hanning Speke in 1858.

VICTORIA FALLS, on the Zambezi River in Africa. Twice as wide and double the depth of Niagara. Its African name is Mosi-oa-tunya, which means 'the smoke that thunders'. Spray from the falls leaps 305 metres into the air and can be seen from 65 kilometres (40 miles) away. It was discovered by David Livingstone in 1871.

LAKE ALBERT, on the border of Zaire and Uganda in Africa, was named by the explorer Samuel Baker in 1864. He was made a Sir for it.

PRINCE ALBERT, a town in Saskatchewan, Canada, started as a church mission station in 1866. It was founded by Rev. James Nesbit.

THE VICTORIA CROSS was invented in 1856. It is the highest award for military bravery. The first crosses were won in the Crimean War. They were made from the bronze of melted-down Russian guns.

VICTORIA, capital of British Columbia, Canada.

VICTORIA ISLAND on Hong Kong.

VICTORIA, a state in Australia.

VICTORIA railway stations in London and Manchester.

 Sir Samuel's brother was dismissed from the army for trying to fondle a governess on a train to Portsmouth. She clung to the outside of the carriage for five miles to escape him.

Check out my scrap-book of cuttings about British Empire battles.

Empire News

CIRCULATION: 10 million

Britain wins drug war
1856

Britain has won the right to sell opium to China, following victory in the second Opium War. The first Opium War has already given Hong Kong island to Britain. The Chinese government opposes the sale of opium because many Chinese are turning into drug addicts, but has at last conceded the right of British drug dealers to sell their product in China.

Crazy cavalry in Crimean carve up
1854

Following a brave but futile charge by 673 members of the Light Brigade against heavy Russian guns, 113 are reported killed, hundreds more wounded or captured, and fifty have returned unharmed. Their commander, Lord Cardigan, is said to be unscathed, and was last heard of having a snack on board his yacht.

Boer war begins
1899

A second war between the British Empire and Dutch settlers, called Boers, has broken out in South Africa. The British Army is expecting a tough time, and is planning a policy of scorched earth and concentration camps.

What a relief
1900

The siege of Mafeking in South Africa by the Boers has finally come to an end. Mafeking has been bravely defended by tough British soldiers commanded by a Colonel Baden-Powell, who held out for 217 days until relief came, using home-made ammunition and guns made from drain-pipes. Baden-Powell is now planning to start the Boy Scouts.

THE INDIAN MUTINY

British rulers were shaken to the core by the Indian Mutiny of 1857. The spark which lit the fuse of the rebellion was when cartridges were given to Indian troops which were coated in grease, made (it was rumoured) from cow or pig fat. These cartridges had to be prepared for firing by being bitten at one end. The cow is a sacred animal to the Hindus and the pig is regarded as unclean by Muslims, so no one was happy.

Indian troops refused to bite the cartridges. Their British officers hanged a few. The troops rioted. They killed their officers, ransacked Delhi, and massacred British men, women and children. For a long time it looked as if the British might be defeated. The cities of Lucknow and Cawnpore were overrun or besieged.

The rebellion was about more than just biting cartridges. It was a revolt against taxation and the laws of the East India Company, which ruled India for Britain. After the mutiny, the British were a lot more careful about how they governed India.

When news of the mutiny reached England, crowds bayed for blood and Victoria was horrified. Seventy thousand troops were sent to India, armed with the new Colt revolvers made popular by the U.S. Cavalry. Revenge was terrible and swift. Rioters were tortured, butchered and blown from cannons.

QUEEN VIC'S BOX OF CHOCS

Victoria wasn't interested in Africa like she was India. After all, nobody made her Empress of Africa. But she still showed an interest...

- She asked the explorer, Stanley, to dinner twice, despite not liking him.

- She sent a gramophone record with a friendly message on it to the Emperor of Ethiopia, with instructions to destroy it after listening to it.

- She followed news from the Boer War very closely. She was upset to learn that the soldiers had been reduced to eating horsemeat. She was very fond of horses.

- She knitted scarves for soldiers and wept over the lists of Boer War casualties. For Christmas 1899, she ordered that every soldier fighting in South Africa be given a box of chocolates with her head embossed on the lid. Unfortunately they arrived late. But many a tale was told later about the chocolate boxes stopping bullets.

- She took more boxes with her when she visited wounded soldiers in London hospitals. One legless soldier declared, "I would rather lose a limb than not get that!" Widows and mothers of dead soldiers buried far from home were often sent the boxes with the dead soldiers' things.

GOODBYE VICTORIA

I'M DREAMING OF A WHITE FUNERAL

Victoria died on the evening of Monday 22 January 1901 at Osborne on the Isle of Wight, with her family gathered around her.

It is said that her last words, after looking out of the window, were, "Oh, Albert....". Did she see Albert at the window? We shall never know.

Victoria loved funerals and she had left detailed instructions about her own. After wearing black mourning for more than thirty years while waiting to join Albert, she intended to go out in style. She wore her white wedding veil in the coffin. Also in the coffin were Albert's dressing gown, a plaster cast of his hand and family photographs. There was also a photograph of John Brown, which Victoria's doctor hid beneath flowers. He didn't want to upset the new king, Edward VII, who had hated the Scotsman.

A BIT OF A HITCH

A boat took the coffin from the Isle of Wight to Portsmouth. It was then put on a train to London. People kneeled by the track as it passed.

In London the coffin was placed on a gun carriage, covered by a white cloth, and pulled by eight white horses from Buckingham Palace to Paddington Station to be put on another train for Windsor.

At Windsor another gun carriage awaited, but there was a problem. As the coffin was placed aboard, the horses kicked and bucked so much that they broke their harness. Meanwhile the front of the procession had marched up Windsor High Street and had to be stopped by a soldier who ran after it.

Back at the station an admiral shouted: "My boys will soon put things right," and got the King's permission to have his sailors drag the gun carriage up the street. The army commander was furious about being told to move his horses and said that the admiral was 'ruining the ceremony'. The sailors rigged up a harness with some telephone cable and heaved the coffin and carriage to the doors of St Georges' Chapel. One up to the navy!

There was a bit of a panic in the tomb at Frogmore while an old servant tried to remember where they'd put Victoria's marble statue all those years ago. They found it eventually and Victoria and Albert were reunited. It snowed as well. The white funeral was complete.

THE END OF AN ERA

Victoria's long reign was over at last. The new King, Edward VII, dismissed the Munshi and the Indian servants. He had the bronze statue of John Brown removed from Windsor, and Brown's room cleared. Victoria's paintings and the collection of things which reminded her of Albert were chucked out, and the rooms redecorated.

The smell of cigar smoke wafted along the palace corridors. The Victorian Age was over. The Edwardian Age was just about to begin – but that's another story!

TOP TEN VICTORIANS

GREAT THINKERS, GREAT BEARDS

CHARLES DICKENS (1812–1870)

OCCUPATION: Novelist.

A dark lank-haired writer and Victorian mega-star. His readings were one of the most popular entertainments of the day.

GOOD POINTS: Dickens was a really gruesome writer and his weird characters are unforgettable. He was very good at describing childhood horrors, as in his books *David Copperfield* and *Great Expectations*. Dickens alerted the Victorian middle classes to the many things he found wrong in the world he knew.

BAD POINTS: His books ramble on a bit. He left his wife, and was terrified of being poor.

ROBERT OWEN (1771-1858)

OCCUPATION: Reformer.

A Scottish industrialist who cared for his workers.

GOOD POINTS: Robert Owen wanted to build a kind of model society around his
factory in New Lanark,
Scotland. He tried to
organise a national
trade union
movement, and start a
perfect colony in
America.

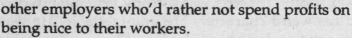

BAD POINT: Owen
was one of those
dreamers who
cause trouble for
other employers who'd rather not spend profits on
being nice to their workers.

KARL MARX (1818-1883)

OCCUPATION: Revolutionary writer.

Karl Marx invented modern Communism, although
he never called himself a Marxist.

GOOD POINTS: Karl Marx was a grey-haired
German-Jewish exile with a big bushy beard, who sat
in the British Museum Library writing about how the
rule of the middle classes would give way to a society
in which there was no exploitation. This was
Communism.

BAD POINTS: His ideas about how to make things better didn't work in practice. He inspired people to set up societies like the Soviet Union, in which people were not only unfree but stayed pretty poor as well.

CHARLES DARWIN (1809-82)

OCCUPATION: Biologist.

A modest, worm-loving biologist, born in Shrewsbury. He extended his interests to finches, turtles and other creatures.

GOOD POINTS: Darwin invented evolution (almost) in his book *Origin of Species*. He argued that all life was descended from the same ancestors and had evolved in different ways. According to Darwin, Man and the monkeys were cousins !

BAD POINTS: Not many. Rather shy. The writer Thomas Huxley had to go round putting forward Darwin's arguments, and called himself 'Darwin's bulldog'.

ALFRED, LORD TENNYSON (1809-1902)

OCCUPATION: Dreamy poet.

Tennyson was a handsome hunk with long locks, who could turn out poems at the drop of a hat.

GOOD POINTS: Tennyson wrote poems which seemed to say that there was a better life somewhere else. He wrote an especially long one called *In Memoriam*, about the death of a friend. This was exactly the sort of poetry Queen Victoria liked.

BAD POINTS: A bit sad. After reading one of his poems you may start crying unexpectedly and have to go to bed early.

RUDYARD KIPLING (1865-1936)

OCCUPATION: Writer.

An adventurous journalist who became a super-star by his own efforts.

GOOD POINTS: Wrote exciting tales about India. Good books include *Kim*, *The Jungle Book* and *The Just So Stories*.

BAD POINTS: He liked to persuade people that the

British Empire was a wonderful thing, which made it more difficult for Britain to let go of it in the next century.

ISAMBARD KINGDOM BRUNEL (1806–1859)

OCCUPATION: Engineer.

A tough hard-worker who pushed out the boundaries of technology.

GOOD POINTS: Isambard Kingdom Brunel was a bold builder of railways, bridges, tunnels and transatlantic ships, including the Great Western (the first steamship to cross the Atlantic) and the Clifton suspension bridge.

BAD POINTS: Not everything worked.

FLORENCE NIGHTINGALE (1820-1910)

OCCUPATION: Nurse.

A dedicated and determined woman, who got what she wanted when she wanted it. She also set an example for millions of women by showing that middle-class women could have a career, and not just be wives.

GOOD POINTS: Florence Nightingale saved many lives by making sure that hospitals were clean and well run. She first came to fame as a nurse during the Crimean War, where she found the hospitals crowded and filthy. Her new rules cut the death rate from 42% to 2.2%.

BAD POINTS: Hard to argue with.

DR BARNADO (1845-1905)

OCCUPATION: Philanthropist (a person who does good).

GOOD POINTS: Dr Thomas Barnardo set up the famous charity homes bearing his name which have given

millions of orphans a better start in life, and took millions of children off the streets.

BAD POINTS: Grumpy. Barnado's homes started off pretty strict by modern standards.

OSCAR WILDE (1854–1900)

OCCUPATION: Writer.

A huge Irish dandy who had a way with words.

GOOD POINTS: Oscar Wilde was funny. He wrote entertaining plays and other stuff which tried to get Victorians to be less serious and enjoy themselves more. For example, when Victorian do-gooders went round saying, "Drink is the curse of the working classes", Wilde turned it around and said: "Work is the curse of the drinking classes". Perhaps the wittiest man ever.

SAD POINT: Wilde was gay (a shocking thing at the time). He was sent to jail and died in exile.

STATE THE DATE

WHAT HAPPENED WHEN?

1837	Queen Victoria crowned
1838	Chartists organise the People's Charter
1839	The Bedchamber Crisis
	The First Opium War begins
1840	Victoria marries Prince Albert
	Penny post is introduced
1842	Mines Act is passed
	Chadwick reports on sanitary conditions
1844	Rochdale Co-op founded
	First telegraph
1845-51	Irish Famine begins
1846	Corn Laws repealed
1847	Communist Manifesto published
1848	Public Health Act
1849	Punjab conquered
1851	The Great Exhibition
1854-6	Crimean War
1857-8	Indian Mutiny
1861	Death of Prince Albert

1863	Bertie marries Alexandra
1864	Albert Memorial built
1868	Trades Union Congress founded
1871	Stanley meets Livingstone
1875	Suez Canal shares bought
1876	Victoria becomes Empress of India

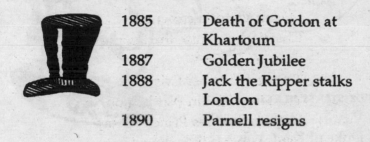

1885	Death of Gordon at Khartoum
1887	Golden Jubilee
1888	Jack the Ripper stalks London
1890	Parnell resigns

1894	Manchester Ship Canal opened
1895	Oscar Wilde trial
1897	Diamond Jubilee
1899-1902	Second Boer War
1900	Labour Party founded
1901	Queen Victoria dies

THE END

GRAND QUIZ

Try my quiz to test your knowledge about Victoria and her times.

QUIZ STARTS HERE...

1. Victoria's father, the Duke of Kent, was...
a) a kindly sort of man
b) the most hated man in the British army
c) a military hero

2. Why did posh girls balance books on their heads?
a) to help them learn the contents
b) because they had no satchels
c) to make them walk better

3. How many children did
   Victoria have?
   a) eleven
   b) nine
   c) thirteen

4. Who wore moleskin
   trousers?
   a) navvies
   b) mole-catchers
   c) Prince Albert

5. Who were the Chartists
   a) early map-makers
   b) a type of industrialist
   c) workers seeking reforms

6. What was a boneshaker?
   a) a machine for making
      fertilizer
   b) a Victorian thug
   c) an early bicycle

7. Who was Amelia Dyer?
   a) an early nurse
   b) someone who opened
      the first nurseries
   c) a baby-murderer

8. What was a bug-hunter?
a) a type of watch
b) someone who robbed drunks
c) a naturalist like Charles Darwin

9 Why did some men wear paper bags?
a) because they were mad
b) as a fashion statement
c) because they were poor

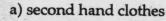

10. What were hand-me-down clothes?
a) second hand clothes
b) ready-to-wear clothes
c) hand-made clothes

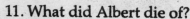

11. What did Albert die of?
a) typhoid
b) cholera
c) over-work

12. What was a gillie?
a) a type of fish
b) a Scottish servant
c) a young girl

13. What were mudlarks?
a) a type of bird
b) a comedy act
c) people who picked coal
   from river mud

14. Who started the modern
    police force?
a) Sir Robert Peel
b) William Gladstone
c) Prince Albert

15. Who talked too much?
a) Disraeli
b) Gladstone
c) John Brown

16. What was the 'white man's burden'?
a) taxes
b) the Industrial Revolution
c) the Empire

Quiz continues over the page...

17. What are Victoria Crosses
    made from?
a) bronze from melted down
   French guns from the
   battle of Waterloo
b) bronze from melted down
   Russian guns from the
   Crimean War
c) gold

18. Who made themselves popular with Queen
    Victoria by putting up a statue of Albert?
a) a patriotic group of mudlarks
b) the town of Wolverhampton
c) the Chartists

See how you scored...

18) b, page 66
17) b, page 102
16) c, page 99
15) b, pages 89 and 90
14) a, page 87
13) c, page 82
12) b, page 68
11) a, page 63
10) b, page 62

9) c, page 59
8) b, page 53
7) c, page 52
6) c, page 35
5) c, page 40
4) a, page 32
3) b, page 23
2) c, page 10
1) b, see page 7

INDEX

READ ON

If you want to know more about Victoria and her times you could see if your local library or bookshop has these books:

THE HISTORY DETECTIVE INVESTIGATES: VICTORIAN CRIME BY PETER CHRISP (HODDER WAYLAND 2002)
The canine history detective, Sherlock Bones, helps you find out about all the crimes committed by those nasty Victorians.

THE HISTORY DETECTIVE INVESTIGATES: VICTORIAN SCHOOL BY RICHARD WOOD (HODDER WAYLAND 2003)
From rules and punishments to classrooms and equipment, discover what schools were really like in the Victorian Age.

GREAT EXPECTATIONS BY CHARLES DICKENS (1861)
Orphan Pip is forced to help the convict Magwitch to escape... Full of crazy characters, this Victorian blockbuster will make you both laugh and cry.

WHO? WHAT? WHEN? VICTORIANS BY BOB FOWKE (HODDER CHILDREN'S BOOKS 2003)
An A to Z of all the important bits you need to know about Victorian Britain.

THE DIARY OF A NOBODY BY GEORGE AND WEEDON GROSSMITH (1894)
The story of Charles Pooter's daily round. Brings the daily existence of the Victorian lower-middle class to life.

QUEEN VICTORIA WAS AMUSED BY ALAN HARDY
(JOHN MURRAY 1976)
Most people think Victoria was a boring old kill-joy.
In fact, she loved dancing till dawn and going to the
fair. Then she met Albert...

A HISTORY OF EVERYDAY THINGS IN ENGLAND
VOLUMES III (1733-1851) AND IV (1851-1914)
BY MARJORIE AND C. H. B. QUENNELL (BATSFORD 1934)
Jam-packed with everything you ever wanted to
know about how the Victorians lived in amazing
detail. This book is a bit old-fashioned, but then so
were the Victorians.

ALL ABOUT THE VICTORIANS BY JANE GOODWIN (HODDER
WAYLAND 2001)
Find out about all the important people and the events
that took place during Queen Victoria's reign.

VICTORIA BY STANLEY WEINTRAUB (HARPER COLLINS
1987)
A really fat book. Loads of interesting snippets.

THE VICTORIANS BY TIM WOOD (LADYBIRD 1994)
Small and slim but with a lot packed in. A good
introduction to the Victorian Age. Lots of colour
pictures.